William Jefferson Clinton

by Sally Lee

Consulting Editor: Gail Saunders-Smith, PhD

Consultant:
Sheila Blackford
Librarian, Scripps Library
Managing Editor, *American President*
Miller Center, University of Virginia

CAPSTONE PRESS
a capstone imprint

Pebble Plus is published by Capstone Press,
1710 Roe Crest Drive, North Mankato, Minnesota 56003.
www.capstonepub.com

Library of Congress Cataloging-in-Publication Data
Lee, Sally.
William Jefferson Clinton / by Sally Lee.
p. cm.—(Pebble plus. Presidential biographies)
Includes bibliographical references and index.
Summary: "Simple text and full-color photographs describe the life of William Jefferson Clinton"—Provided by
publisher.
ISBN 978-1-4296-8585-6 (library binding)
ISBN 978-1-62065-321-0 (ebook PDF)
1. Clinton, Bill, 1946– —Juvenile literature. 2. Presidents—United States—Biography—Juvenile literature. I. Title.
E886.L44 2013
973.929092—dc23
[B]   2011049863

Editorial Credits
Erika L. Shores, editor; Sarah Bennett, designer; Wanda Winch, media researcher; Kathy McColley,
    production specialist

Photo Credits
AP Images: Ron Edmonds, 19; Courtesy; The William J. Clinton Presidential Library, cover, 1, 5, 7, 11, 13; Getty
Images Inc: Arnold Sachs, 9; Library of Congress: Prints and Photographs Division, 17; Newscom: Joe Sohm Visions
of America, 15, RTR/Swoan Parker, 21

Note to Parents and Teachers

The Presidential Biographies series supports national history standards related to people and
culture. This book describes and illustrates the life of William Jefferson Clinton. The images
support early readers in understanding the text. The repetition of words and phrases helps early
readers learn new words. This book also introduces early readers to subject-specific vocabulary
words, which are defined in the Glossary section. Early readers may need assistance to read
some words and to use the Table of Contents, Glossary, Read More, Internet Sites, and Index
sections of the book.

Printed in the United States of America in Stevens Point, Wisconsin.
072013   007607R

Table of Contents

Early Years

William Jefferson Clinton loves people and politics. Known as Bill, the future president was born August 19, 1946. Bill's mother, Virginia, named him William Jefferson Blythe after his father who had died.

born in Hope, Arkansas

1946

Young Bill Clinton in 1952

At first, Bill lived with
his grandparents. His grandfather
taught him to read.
Later, Virginia married
Roger Clinton. Bill took
his stepfather's last name.

→ born in Hope,
Arkansas

1946

Bill, Virginia, and Bill's half-brother, Roger, in 1958

Young Adult

In high school Bill went to

Boys Nation in Washington, D.C.

He spent a week learning about

the government and even met

President John F. Kennedy.

After that trip, Bill knew

he wanted a life in politics.

born in Hope, Arkansas

1946

9

Bill began Yale Law School
in 1970. He met Hillary Rodham,
another student who shared
his love of politics. They married
in 1975. Their daughter, Chelsea,
was born five years later.

born in Hope,
Arkansas

marries
Hillary Rodham

1946   1970   1975

enters Yale
Law School

Life in Arkansas

Bill first ran for office in Arkansas. After serving as attorney general, he was elected governor in 1978. At age 32, he was one of the youngest governors ever.

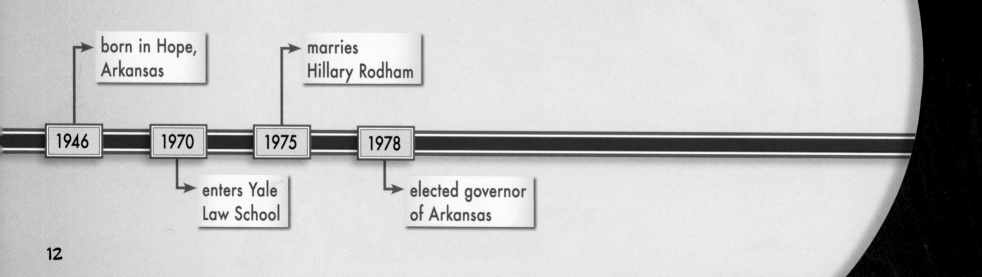

| 1946 | 1970 | 1975 | 1978 |

born in Hope, Arkansas

marries Hillary Rodham

enters Yale Law School

elected governor of Arkansas

As governor, Bill worked
to improve the schools and
the economy in Arkansas.
After 12 years as governor,
he decided to run
for U.S. president.

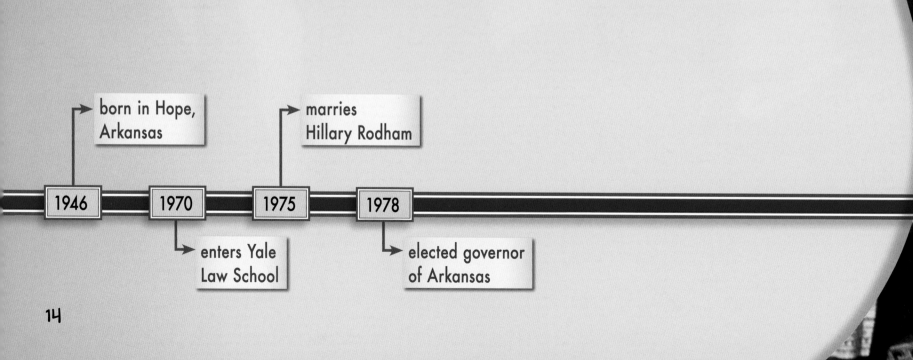

born in Hope,
Arkansas

marries
Hillary Rodham

1946

1970

1975

1978

enters Yale
Law School

elected governor
of Arkansas

President Clinton

Bill Clinton became the 42nd U.S. president on January 20, 1993. As president, he hoped to improve health care. He asked Hillary to lead a group to change the health care system. But the plan did not pass Congress.

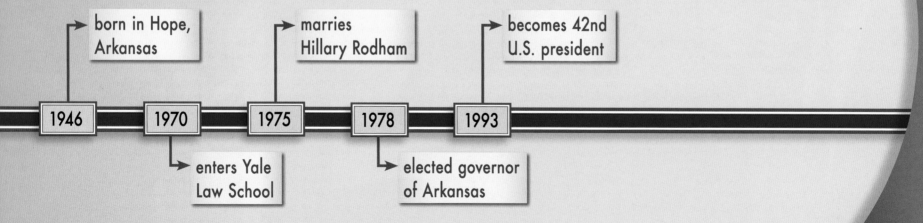

| 1946 | 1970 | 1975 | 1978 | 1993 |

born in Hope, Arkansas

marries Hillary Rodham

becomes 42nd U.S. president

enters Yale Law School

elected governor of Arkansas

When Bill became president,

the government was in debt.

Many people needed jobs.

He worked with Congress

to cut spending

and improve the economy.

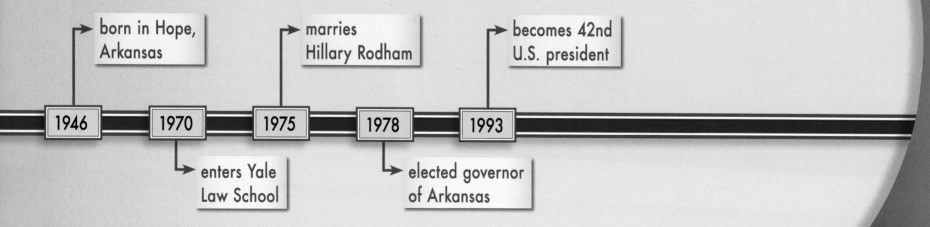

born in Hope,
Arkansas

marries
Hillary Rodham

becomes 42nd
U.S. president

1946   1970   1975   1978   1993

enters Yale
Law School

elected governor
of Arkansas

A Balanced Budget

That Protects Our Families, Invests in Our People
and Cuts Taxes for Middle Class Families

After serving eight years,

Bill left office in January 2001.

He began raising money for

disaster relief and other causes

around the world. He has never

stopped caring about people.

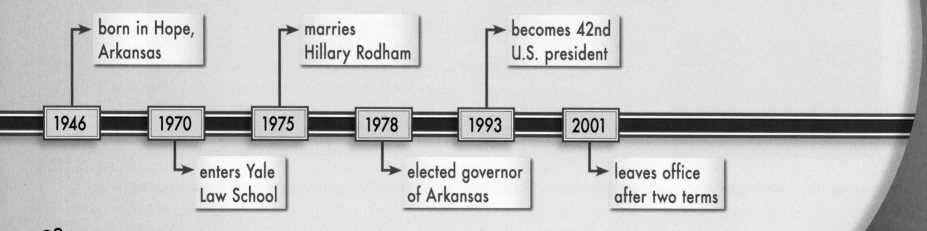

born in Hope, Arkansas

marries Hillary Rodham

becomes 42nd U.S. president

1946   1970   1975   1978   1993   2001

enters Yale Law School

elected governor of Arkansas

leaves office after two terms

Glossary

attorney general—the chief lawyer for a state or country

Boys Nation—a yearly event run by the American Legion where two boys chosen from each state learn about the national government

Congress—the branch of the U.S. government that is elected to make laws; Congress is made up of the Senate and the House of Representatives

debt—owing money

disaster—a sudden event that causes a lot of damage, such as an earthquake, flood, hurricane, or tornado

economy—the system of how money is made and used within a particular country or area

politics—the work or study of government

Read More

Lee, Sally. *Hillary Clinton.* First Ladies. Mankato, Minn.: Capstone Press, 2011.

Peppas, Lynn. *Election Day.* Celebrations in My World. Ontario, Canada: Crabtree Publishing Company, 2010.

Rumsch, BreAnn. *Bill Clinton.* The United States Presidents. Edina, Minn.: ABDO Pub. Co., 2009.

Internet Sites

FactHound offers a safe, fun way to find Internet sites related to this book. All of the sites on FactHound have been researched by our staff.

Here's all you do:

Visit *www.facthound.com*

Type in this code: 9781429685856

Check out projects, games and lots more at
www.capstonekids.com

Index

Word Count: 271
Grade: 1
Early-Intervention Level: 21